Wisdom & the Dreamer

Wisdom & the Dreamer

Achieving Fulfillment in the Arts

by

KRISTEN THIES

WEST WIND FINE ART

Coeur d'Alene · Idaho

2006

Wisdom & the Dreamer: Achieving Fulfillment in the Arts
© Kristen Thies 2005

Foreword by Sandra Carpenter.
Paintings © Timothy R. Thies 2005.
Edited by Corinna Fales.
All photographs © Kristen and Timothy R. Thies 2005

Additional paintings used by permission from Richard Schmid:
  "Portrait of Kristen Thies: For Kristen the Dreamer" © Richard Schmid 2001 (cover image); "Portrait of Timothy R. Thies © Richard Schmid 2001; "April Thaw" © Richard Schmid 2000; "Cliffs at Martha's Vineyard" © Richard Schmid 2002; "Peonies & Laurel Leaves" © Richard Schmid 2003; "Sunday Afternoon" © Richard Schmid 2003.
Additional paintings used by permission from Nancy Guzik:
  "Daffodils" © Nancy Guzik 1998; "Zorro" © Nancy Guzik 1999; "Openings" © Nancy Guzik 2003; "Janice" © Nancy Guzik 2005.

Published by: West Wind Fine Art, LLC
        P.O. Box 3390
        Coeur d'Alene, Idaho 83816
        Telephone: 802-297-3771 Fax: 802-297-3326
        Web site: www.WestWindFineArt.com
        Email: cornerstoneorders@adelphia.net

ISBN 978-09763655-01
Library of Congress Control Number: 2005935775

This book was prepared for printing by Stephen Stinehour, at Stinehour Wemyss Editions, Lunenburg, Vermont, and printed in China. First printing, June 2006

Portrait of Timothy R. Thies. Oil, 12" × 16" by Richard Schmid. ▶

FOR MY HUSBAND, TIMOTHY R. THIES

With gratitude for his vision, integrity and our love.
His passion for the arts and his light-filled paintings endlessly
inspire my soul.

Contents

ACKNOWLEDGEMENTS

Thank you to Richard Schmid and Nancy Guzik for permission to reproduce their exquisite paintings and for their invitation to share their journey in the arts.

Gratitude and thank you to Corinna Fales for her excellent editorial services. and substantive advice.

To Sandra Carpenter for her insightful Foreword, *Looking Behind the Scenes.*

To Paul Soderberg for his perceptive bios of Timothy and me.

To Linda Laflamme for her expert advice and concept editing services.

In addition, immense appreciation to our patrons and friends for allowing me to quote their thoughts on collecting fine art.

To George Carlson and Richard Schmid for sharing their invaluable insights on fine art.

To my mother, Patti Williams, for her love and encouragement throughout my life.

We are extremely grateful for permission to reproduce copyright material listed in the "Notes" following each chapter. While every reasonable effort has been made to trace copyright holders, the publishers would be pleased to hear from any not acknowledged here.

Looking Behind the Scenes

"*WISDOM & THE DREAMER* gently nudges you forward into your life as an artist, encouraging you to follow your dreams and your path—whatever they may be," says Timothy Thies of his wife's book.

It's this gentle encouragement, combined with sound marketing and business advice, as well as a variety of handy tools and resources that makes this book so unique in the art world. The information is all offered by Kristen and based on her 25-year career in the arts. And because *Wisdom & The Dreamer* is also Timothy's story, there's perhaps no one better to comment from his behind-the-scenes vantage point on what this book is about. "The creative process from start to finish is here," he continues. "It's a great read. I learned a lot about myself as well as the art field by reading this."

This book encapsulates what it is to be an artist from a variety of viewpoints. With art experience ranging from working as a successful gallery director to being the wife of an artist and also the marketing manager for painter Richard Schmid, Kristen understands the nuances of trying to make a living as an artist. The success the Thies' now share is the result of long years of frustration and failure, years when they didn't expect to survive at all in the art world.

"There's a sense of satisfaction when you realize the difficulty you've been through and that you've survived," says Timothy. "Looking back, you understand what happened, why it happened and how you've succeeded. We're very grateful for all we have now. It feels like a dream that we're where we are."

Initially this was going to be a book on marketing, based on a presentation Kristen gave to an art group and the countless requests she received for help with marketing from other top artists. But as Kristen began working on the book, it made her and Timothy see how far they'd come in their own artistic journey. This realization made them want to share the wealth of their entire experience. "We decided that we didn't just want to give tools for marketing, but also share our life journey," says Timothy. "Thus this is a life lesson manual as well as an art book. There are so many layers of information that you can get out of it."

As for the title, Timothy says that to him it refers to the idea that all the knowledge you can gather is just knowledge until you can integrate it back into who you are. Only then does it become wisdom. The dreamer aspect has to do with thinking about where you want to go with your painting. "Where do you see yourself? Do you dare to look at a John Singer Sargent painting and say 'how can I do this better?' This book isn't about becoming famous, unless that's what you want to become. Rather it's about realizing your dreams as defined by who you are."

Timothy adds that he's proud of Kristen's vision and how she created this book. There is much greater potential for understanding art and the art world as the information here can provide a multi-dimensional experience. "With Kristen's book, the reader can go within themselves for another layer of understanding the information as well as look at paintings—some favorite paintings that relate to the mood and content. The book gives the reader the visual experience and the possibility of a mental and emotional experience.

"It's her truth as she sees it and her experience," he continues. "She reveals herself and her life and how she got through some of the difficulties and succeeded. Kristen shared this information so that other people could know how to present themselves in a professional manner."

There's no exact formula for how many miles of canvas you have to paint, how many books you have to read and masterworks you have to study to become a successful artist, concludes Timothy. That's a different journey for each artist. But this book will give you a unique inside view of what it's like to go through the process and perhaps provide you with a few tools to make your own path easier to travel.

— SANDRA CARPENTER

SANDRA CARPENTER is a Stockholm, Sweden-based writer specializing in the arts, as well as the former editorial director and editor of *The Artist's Magazine.*

Rose Archway. Oil, 30" × 24" © Timothy R. Thies ▶

WISDOM *&* THE DREAMER
Achieving Fulfillment in the Arts

PART I

Portrait of Kristen Thies: For Kristen the Dreamer. Oil, 16" × 20" © Richard Schmid

I
Wisdom and the Dreamer

*I*N EARLY 1997, RICHARD SCHMID hired me to find a publisher for his third book, *Alla Prima: Everything I Know About Painting*—with his enviable credentials, I thought it would be an easy task. Armed with imagination, research from a dozen books on the publishing industry, and immense determination, I wrote and designed the most beautiful and comprehensive book proposal that I could conceive. My prototype consisted of an overview of the book, several sample chapters written by Richard Schmid, twelve color copies of his paintings, a marketing proposal, a short bio, and a list of selected exhibitions. After three months of work, I presented my proposal to Richard. To my delight and immense relief, he loved it!

With his approval, I then reproduced the proposal and mailed the packets to four highly respected art-book publishers, and waited the customary three to four weeks for their reply. The first proposal arrived in our mailbox unopened. The other editors returned the proposal along with more considerate rejection letters that read something like this: "Although we feel Mr. Schmid's work is quite beautiful, his book is much too selective for our market . . . We wish you good luck with your endeavor."

I was surprised and a bit dismayed by their rejections, but I maintained my resolve. Since I knew that their "selective market" was comprised of artists, I decided to speak to Richard about the alternative route: self-publishing. It is very important to remember, when one decides to become an artist of any kind—author, sculptor, filmmaker, etc.—that failure is not an option!

Richard was also undaunted and asked me to proceed. So, I located a fine-art book printer in Loveland, only an hour's drive from his studio in the mountains of Colorado. Then, with his attorney's counsel and my assistance, Richard formed his own publishing house—known today as Stove Prairie Press, LLC.

As his literary agent, I began the task of designing a marketing plan complete with full-page ads and media packets. I then registered his title with the US Library of Congress and applied for the ISBN. During this process, Richard called one day and asked if West Wind Fine Art, the business I own with my husband and partner, Timothy R. Thies, might be interested in becoming his new company's exclusive distributor.

Fogged In. Oil, 18" × 24" © Timothy R. Thies

In less than a year, all of the production details fell into place, and in January of 1998, several thousand copies of his new book were ready to market.

To date, *Alla Prima* is in its seventh printing and has been sold directly to artists in more than thirty-seven countries. It sits on shelves of American libraries and bookstores and has graced the gift shops in the Metropolitan Museum of Art and the Butler Institute of American Art in Youngstown, Ohio.

In the ensuing years, I have corresponded with hundreds of artists and collectors by phone, fax, email, and the US mail. As Richard Schmid's chief correspondent, I received countless requests from artists longing to study with him. Surprisingly, many painters also asked his advice on dealing with gallery owners and earning a living in the art world. As a result of my marketing expertise and association with Richard, other artists began to ask for my advice.

Daffodils. Oil, 20" × 30" © Nancy Guzik, 2003.

When I first started writing *Wisdom & The Dreamer*, I wondered if anyone would be interested. After a lot of deliberation, I am convinced that it is indeed worthwhile: after all, I mused, hadn't several prominent painters asked me for tips on marketing their own art?

In time however, the book's real purpose evolved. In the process of writing and living my life, I've come to realize that we all need many other skills in order to succeed. Becoming a success in the art world involves more than dreaming about it, and quite a bit more than a huge advertising budget (though having money always helps).

Since childhood, I have been called a dreamer, but in order to achieve my dreams I've been forced to learn patience and perseverance. I've also had to learn that having talent isn't always appreciated or even recognized. Unfortunate and sometimes downright miserable circumstances taught me the importance of adopting a professional attitude, no matter what.

Timothy Thies and I have been on an artistic journey since we met in 1980, and during that time, we have experienced immense joy and extreme despair. I now regard

Lifting Fog. Oil, 30" × 40" © Timothy R. Thies

life's most difficult experiences as my best teachers—for me, wisdom dawned a season (or one might call it a set-back) at a time. With each painful incident, I've been forced to clarify why I feel compelled to express the beauty inherent in my soul. Likewise, Timothy has been forced to question the purpose of going on, despite rejection from shows, gallery owners—even his peers.

Countless times I've wondered why fine art is so important to humanity. Why do millions of people visit the Metropolitan Museum of Art each year? And most perplexing, why do I feel a responsibility to help preserve this fascinating, seven-hundred-year-old tradition of knowledge known as representational art? After all, it's the twenty-first century and we live in the fast-paced race of the electronic age.

In an effort to find answers to my questions, I asked several respected artists and writers for the meaning and purpose of art in their lives. And in order to overcome the sadness caused by each rejection, I retreated to my room to consult the timeless works of William Shakespeare, Sir Alfred Lord Tennyson, President Lincoln, and the great Lebanese poet Kahlil Gibran, to name but a few. I also spent hours researching the lives of American artists from the nineteenth and twentieth centuries. Their words and the beauty of their work fortified me and helped justify my commitment.

And when my life was threatened by illness, I found solace in the wisdom of the ages—from the master teacher, Jesus Christ. In time, as my healing took place and the fog of doubt and fear lifted, it became easier to envision a new path. I have emerged with more confidence and a renewed commitment to share some of the insights that Tim and I learned along the way.

Wisdom & The Dreamer, then, is the result of our journey. It's a compilation of the experiences, musings, inspiration, and work of two entrepreneurs, from amateur to award-winning artist, and from novice to successful gallery owner. Even now, I'm sometimes amazed at my career because I really do represent one of the world's finest living masters—artist and author, Richard Schmid—in addition to the work of two other highly respected artists, Nancy Guzik and Timothy R. Thies.

Mother Teresa said, "In this life we cannot do great things; only small things with great love."[1] So I offer this book with great love in the hope that something within its pages will help kindle your own artistic commitment. As Robert Henri said, "Everything depends on it."[2]

NOTES

1. Malcomb Muggeridge, *Something Beautiful for God* (copyright The Mother Teresa Committee 1971.)

2. Robert Henri, *The Art Spirit* (Colorado: Westview Press. 1984).

2
Overcoming Rejection

But like a compass seeking north
There lives in me a still, sure, spirit part.
Clouds of doubt are cut asunder
By the lighting and the thunder
Shining from the compass of my heart. [1]

—DAVID CROSBY

WHENEVER TIMOTHY'S WORK was rejected from major art shows, or when gallery owners neglected to send payment for his paintings (which seemed to occur just about the time our rent was due), I needed a way to overcome my despair. "It's time to give up," Tim would say in utter frustration. But in a day or two, we would somehow pick ourselves up, re-evaluate our options, and continue. Rejection can be a wonderful catalyst for working even harder to perfect one's skills, and it became a primary motivation for my desire to write.

For years I wondered how—if ever—I would reach my goals. Owning a fine art gallery and becoming a professional writer seemed far from reach when we were having difficulty just paying our bills. During trying times, I'd take a long walk in the woods or sit by the ponds near our home. On rainy days, I'd simply escape to my room.

There, in the quiet of my solitude, I'd find strength from the writings of great poets and artists, such as the revered nineteenth-century painter and teacher Robert Henri, who urged others to continue, no matter what!

When he died in 1929, Henri (who, along with Thomas Eakins and William Merritt Chase, had shaped a generation of painters through his effective teaching style) knew that the modern art movement was overshadowing representational art; as a result, abstract art would virtually obliterate representational work, and eventually even lead to its removal from art school instruction.

In response, Henri wrote, "All any man can do is to add his fragment to the whole, no man can be final, but he can record his progress—what he leaves is so much for others to step on or stones to avoid." He also admonished other young artists to "not let the fact that things are not made for you or that conditions are not as they should be [stop you]. Go on anyway. Everything depends on those who go on anyway."[2]

Henri's unwavering commitment to keeping representational painting alive inspired me, because abstract art does not capture the spiritual or emotional essence of nature in the same way. But what exactly did he mean?

Several passages from William Innes Homer's notable book *Robert Henri and His Circle*, gave me more insight into his resolve. In particular:

> Teaching for Henri was not just a way of earning a living; it was a duty he shouldered voluntarily because he believed he had a mission in fostering the growth of art in his native country. His profound faith in the progress of American art, both present and future—undoubtedly inspired by Walt Whitman—was readily transmitted to his students and gave many of them the courage to pursue the difficult business of painting in the face of public indifference."[3]

Robert Henri taught his students to respect fine art by insisting that "the art student constantly be aware of the purpose of his work, which should be 'the presentation of ideas of value,' such as religion, philosophy, or the 'great conditions in life.' Henri believed that art had a responsibility to society. So, the art-for-art's-sake viewpoint was totally irrelevant and useless."[3]

More of Henri's insights appear later in Part II. But suffice it to say for now that I have accepted Henri's advice, and vow not to abandon my dreams, because I firmly believe that the unspoken language of fine art evokes a spiritual and emotional connection with the viewer that represents a truly valuable accomplishment for the artist.

While researching the topic of rejection, I found many great painters whose works failed to win awards in the salons of the nineteenth century. One of these was Jules Bastien-Lepage. According to the October 1924 issue of *The Mentor*, Lepage's painting, *Joan of Arc, the Maid of Orleans*:

> . . . was much discussed when first exhibited, but to the artist's chagrin, it failed to win a medal. He suffered many disappointments. Several times when he competed for medals or for the Prix de Rome, with the fond hope of pleasing his family and friends, he failed to win. His painting was not conservative enough for the judges, but he had the solace of knowing he had the support of his fellow students. But in the course of years, *Joan of Arc, the Maid of Orleans* prevailed against those who originally found fault with it, and the public at large adopted the canvas as their own.[4]

Critics once said that the painting was too full of details. Today, *Joan of Arc, the Maid of Orleans* hangs in the Metropolitan Museum of Art, and the average observer finds in these very details a remarkable combination of draftsmanship and storytelling. Nearly 127 years after he painted it in the small French village of his birth, Lepage's magnificent oil still inspires viewers and conveys his love for the legend of one of France's most revered heroines.

So please take heart if you are experiencing rejection. The voice of the critic can be unkind, but I believe if one makes an honest attempt to create a work of art and it fails to win an award—or, even more demoralizing, is juried out of a show—it's not necessarily the fault of the painting or the artist. Perhaps the juror was a novice or simply having a tough time sifting through hundreds of trays filled with slides.

To further illustrate my point, I offer the following true story. A painting by Richard Schmid was rejected by a New England show. The exhibition was held in a prestigious New Hampshire museum, and his oil was initially accepted. When the painting arrived, however, the museum's director immediately shipped it back with an accompanying letter of apology that conveyed his regrets. He said the Schmid painting was so good that it would make the other entries look inferior! Obviously, the curatorial department didn't know who Schmid is, or the value of his work. Subsequently, I advertised and sold the rejected painting, *April Thaw*, for $60,000, and the quintessential New England snow scene now hangs in a renowned private collection.

Every representational painting expresses a story, and the seed of one by my husband, Timothy, began during our visit to the Metropolitan Museum of Art. We were so inspired by the work of the nineteenth-century sculptor Augustus Saint-Gaudens that we felt compelled to visit his former estate and studio in Cornish, New Hampshire, which is known today as The Saint-Gaudens National State Park. It was late March and the museum was closed, but it was a glorious day, so we decided to walk around the property. When we first encountered the *Shaw Memorial* behind a grove of tall hedges, I was completely overwhelmed. The monument—a tribute to Colonel Robert Gould Shaw and the 54th regiment, the first all-volunteer troop of African American soldiers during the Civil War—gleamed in the afternoon sun. Tim and I were quite moved, especially since we had just watched the film *Glory.*

After experiencing the beauty and power of the bronze, Timothy was filled by an indescribable force to depict the sculpture in oil, though he had never been interested in painting a Civil War piece. As a result, he painted *Ashes to Ashes, Dust to Dust* (which to date has received rejection notices from two exhibitions) and has said of it:

April Thaw. Oil, 24" × 40" © Richard Schmid, 1999.

There are a few moments in an artist's life when a painting seems to paint itself and even fewer times when the energy feels so lively or so powerful that it goes beyond understanding or description. I have never been guided to paint or directed to paint a piece of sculpture before. Even now, I still experience the depth of its significance and when I stand in front of my painting, I'm filled with emotion.

After an experience like that, rejection hardly seems relevant. But according to Timothy, there are some benefits:

Rejection has helped me strive to become a better painter and it has made me more humble. It has forced me to re-evaluate my work and to take note of my weaknesses in order to improve. It is quite easy to become negative, to trash the juror, the show itself, or the award winners, but what purpose does that serve? I've found that if one wants to move forward in life or in one's art, inner reflection is the key. I ask myself: did I do the absolute best painting I was capable of at the time? What are the real reasons for submitting slides to a show? Is it to win an award or to stroke my ego so I can say I've shown my work with the top artists? I hate rejection, but it's a worthwhile experience to honestly ask yourself if your paintings are really ready to show with the best of the best.

Augustus Saint-Gaudens had no way of knowing that his masterpiece would so powerfully inspire another artist in the twenty-first century. Nevertheless, his masterpiece created a lasting connection between the artist and the viewer that—simply put—is the real value of representational art, even if some critics don't agree. "If one achieves what one sets out to accomplish in a painting or a piece of sculpture, the piece is already a success," says Thies.

Rejection is only validated if the experience inhibits or stifles one's creative vision. Therefore, I've come to the conclusion that rejection may serve the artist in improving their work. And *Ashes to Ashes, Dust to Dust* hangs in a special alcove in our home and graces the memory of the fallen soldiers who fought for the freedoms they believed in.

Now, whenever I'm faced with rejection, I recite Eleanor Roosevelt's potent words of wisdom: "Nobody can make you feel inferior without your consent."[5]

NOTES *&* ACKNOWLEDGEMENTS

1. David Crosby, *Compass,* Copyright 1986 Sony/ATV Songs LLC, Stay Straight Music. All rights administered by Sony/ATV Music Publishing, 8 Music Square West, Nashville, TN 37203. All rights reserved. Used by permission.

2. Robert Henri*, The Art Spirit* (Colorado, Westview Press, 1984. p. unknown, p. 14). Used by permission.

3. William Innes Homer, *Robert Henri and His Circle* (New York: Cornell University Press, Sage House; published by Hacker Art Books, 1988), p.158 and 159. Used by permission of William Homer.

4. W. D. Moffat, "The Story of a Picture: Joan of Arc, by Bastien-Lepage*," The Mentor,* October 1924 (Originally published by Crowell Publishing in 1924), p. 48 and 49.

5. Eleanor Roosevelt, *The Wisdom of Eleanor Roosevelt,* ed. Donald Wigal (New York: Citadel Press, Kensington Publishing 2003), p. 10, quotation 23. Used by permission.

6. *Augustus Saint-Gaudens: 1848–1907, A Master of American Sculpture,* the catalog (Cornish, New Hampshire: Saint Gaudens National Historical Site, 1999) p. 130, 131. Used by permission.

7. Lincoln Kirstein, *Lay This Laurel* (New York: Eakins Press Foundation, 1973), Essay IV. Used with permission, copyright © Eakins Press Foundation, 1995. Used by permission.

Ashes to Ashes, Dust to Dust. ▶
Oil, 28" × 22" © Timothy R. Thies.
Inspired by the Shaw Memorial.

12

Over the course of thirteen years, Augustus Saint-Gaudens worked on the memorial in his New York studio. The monument, a tribute to Colonel Robert Gould Shaw and the 54th Regiment, the first African-American regiment during the civil war was unveiled in Boston (Massachusetts) on Friday, May 21, 1897. Colonel Shaw and many of his regiment were killed leading the assault on Fort Wagner, Charleston Harbor, South Carolina, on July 18, 1863.[6]

© Saint Gaudens National Historical Site.

Portrait Sketch of
Augustus Saint-Gaudens.
Charcoal, 17" × 15"
© Timothy R. Thies

After completing thirteen years of work on the *Shaw Memorial*, Saint-Gaudens wrote:

It was the extraordinary opportunity, the interest of the task, and my enthusiasm, that led to a development far beyond what was expected of me. And I held it a great joy to be able to carry out my idea as I wished . . .

My own delay I excuse on the grounds that a sculptor's work endures for so long that it is next to a crime for him to neglect to do everything that lies in his power to execute a result that will not be a disgrace . . . [7]

Used with permission, copyright © Eakins Press Foundation, 1995.

3
Creativity versus the Business Mind

A man of humanity is one who, in seeking to establish himself,
Finds a foothold for others and who,
Desiring attainment for himself helps others to attain.

—CONFUCIUS

WE ARE SITTING BY THE SEA as waves crash on the glistening shore and sea gulls glide high above the ancient cliffs of Aquinnah, which means "under the cliffs" or "land under the hill." Settled by the Native American Wampanoag tribe more than five thousand years ago, Aquinnah is the most remote part of the peninsula and the least populated town on Martha's Vineyard.

As I write, Richard, Nancy, and Timothy are deeply immersed in painting the colors and shapes of the landscape, which is quite a challenge due to the subtle atmospheric conditions and ever-changing light. It is the first week of October and we are visiting the Vineyard to celebrate life, art, and Richard Schmid's birthday.

I love spending hours near the ocean; undisturbed, my thoughts flow freely like the clouds. I'm filled with gratitude for the many gifts in my life: my incredible relationship with my husband, creativity, art, and especially for our friendship and professional association with Richard Schmid and Nancy Guzik.

For some, however, the relationship between artist and art dealer can be quite challenging. Before owning my own business, I worked in two other art galleries, and witnessed struggles between the artists and the businessmen and women who were driven by the bottom line. I also attended numerous artist parties where discussions invariably turned to blame. Disgruntled by poor sales, some accused their art dealers of taking too much commission when a painting finally sold. They also criticized dealers for choosing to only advertise work by a select group of top-selling artists, as well as for their indifference to promoting works by lesser known painters and sculptors. Some artists even belittled the owners and sales personnel for knowing nothing about fine art.

Conversely, I listened to perplexed art dealers commiserate because they didn't comprehend why *their* artists objected to painting another piece like the one that had

Cliffs at Martha's Vineyard. Oil, 8" × 16" © Richard Schmid, 2002.

Fisherman's Rock. Oil, 24" × 30" © Timothy R. Thies, 2002.

16

just sold. In recent years, their most frequent complaint has been that the artists they nurtured have saved their best works for major museum exhibitions. Some dealers also blame artists for not supplying their salon with enough new paintings, and for their ignorance of the art gallery business — on and on it goes.

I'm no expert on relationships, but I've grown weary of these constant complaints. Observing life in the art world from different points of view is confounding. So the words from Joni Mitchell's timeless song, "Both Sides, Now," best describe my perspective:

> I've looked at life from both sides now
> From up and down, and still somehow
> It's life's illusions I recall
> I really don't know life at all.[1]

I don't have all the answers, but I do know this: art is a business, and it's exasperating sometimes. But when it works, it's one of the most fulfilling ventures in life. Fine art is a lifetime career, and it becomes what one makes of it. So playing the blame-game is a waste of time. Like all serious businesses, the field of art can be extremely difficult. But one *can* succeed.

All you need as a professional artist is a tremendous desire to do what you most love to do: painting, sculpting, etc. It just takes determination, perseverance, and creativity to earn a living from it. But a positive, light-hearted approach and a few good marketing skills definitely make it possible.

It also takes some quiet introspection. I believe the time has come for us to recognize and acknowledge that many artists live in a state of victim-hood. So it's essential to banish the starving artist/poor me syndrome once and for all! (More of my personal insights on this are covered in the chapter, "Introspection and Infinite Hope.")

Do I hear you ask if it's really worth the effort? After taking a deep sigh, I listen to the melody of Joni's song playing in my mind. Her words go on, just like time:

> It's life's illusions I recall
> I really don't know life at all.[1]

But after twenty-two years, I have acquired a few good survival skills. And writing this book is one of them.

My aim is to help you take responsibility for your *own* fine art career. If we are to grow as artists, I believe we need to develop both sides of our brains.

Room with a View. Oil, 30" × 40" © Timothy R. Thies, 2001.

So I've provided a sample agreement—with important points to consider when drafting legal documents. These are designed to promote good will between the creative mind and the business mind—because both sides really *do* need each other. (For more advice on self-promotion, and resources valuable to artists, check out Part II.)

And one chapter, "Collectors and the Unspoken Language of Art," deals with one of the most important aspects of being a professional artist: finding the balance between pleasing the viewer and pleasing oneself. It's an ongoing challenge, but well worth trying. Experience has shown me that pure creative expression is always fulfilling, especially when a bond develops between the artist, his or her work, the dealer, and the all-important art collector.

Being an artist is a gift with a high spiritual calling, and society needs the uplift that the beauty of fine art offers, especially since the tragedy of 9-11. Fine art works are compelling, and if a painting is done well enough, it satisfies the soul's longing to experience more than the mundane routine of daily life. For example, one collector friend described her love of Richard Schmid's paintings this way: "You help us to really see the beauty in an old tree log, in the forest, and even the most simple things of life."

Paul Soderberg, the novelist and former editor of *Art-Talk*, quoted me in an article he wrote on art hype for the April 2005 issue. It was a wonderful opportunity to share my opinion, and I live by what I said:

> Beyond "value" there is "worth." We've always believed that fine art possesses much more worth than its monetary value—especially great art, because it has the power to inspire and uplift, and it's priceless. Great art is just like a majestic mountain or a stunning sunset that makes you grateful to be alive: you can't put a price tag on it.[2]

NOTES

1. Joni Mitchell, *Both Sides, Now,* words and music by Joni Mitchell ©1967 (Renewed) Siquomb Publishing Corp. Copyright assigned to Crazy Crow Music, used by permission of Alfred Publishing Co., Inc. All rights reserved.

2. Paul Soderberg, "Art Hype" (Scottsdale: *Art-Talk,* April 2005).

Autumn Light. Oil, 30" × 24" © Timothy R. Thies, 2005.

4
Introspection and Infinite Hope

LETTING GO OF THE "POOR ME" AND "STARVING ARTIST" SYNDROME

We must constantly build dikes of courage to hold back the flood of fear.
We must accept finite disappointment, but we must never lose infinite hope.
Only when it is dark enough can you see the stars.[1]

—MARTIN LUTHER KING, JR.

*W*EBSTER'S DICTIONARY (1971) defines rejection as "the state of being rejected; to reject means to refuse to acknowledge, to hear, receive grant or consider." Throughout history, artists have experienced this uncomfortable state. But if we look a bit deeper, being thrust into an experience over which we have no control can lead us in new directions. Growth is a process, and detours such as rejection, lack of recognition, loss, and illness are simply a part of the journey of life.

I experienced one of the most difficult detours in my life after a routine medical exam in 1991 when an M.D. told me that I needed exploratory surgery—"just in case"—to rule out the likelihood of ovarian cancer. As you might expect, I needed encouraging and hopeful words to contain my fear. Aside from receiving expert medical advice (allopathic, ayurvedic, naturopathic, and chiropractic), introspection became one of the most valuable tools in helping me cope with my illness and calm my fears.

It took me a couple of years to fully recover my health because I really tried to follow a natural path. Though the ovarian cyst I had turned out to be benign, I eventually opted to undergo surgery because I was tired of feeling tired! During this period, I learned that the path to wholeness follows its own course: like a mountain stream, the water sometimes runs swiftly over boulders and moss-covered rocks—then suddenly flows into deep, still, and silent pools. Similarly, I came to cherish the quiet, introspective side of my nature because the inner strength I gained helped to restore my spirit while my body healed.

The long healing process also forced me to clearly define my personal goals. In college, I had majored in apparel design, and for several years after graduation, I was happy in my chosen field. I became accustomed to being a designer and identified my-

Woodland Falls. Oil, 30" × 40" © Timothy R. Thies, 2004.

self that way, but never felt that the commercial work I did for a living was important. Because my job forced me to follow the dictates of the highly superficial fashion industry, I didn't feel truly creative. Eventually, my angst and the constant deadlines contributed to an imbalance that weakened my immune system. Though I never want to face "dis-ease" again, the experience was really a blessing in disguise: I now realize that the lack of genuine creative fulfillment was a major cause of my illness.

Ultimately, introspection became an inner force for positive change. I longed for perfect health, but it eluded me until I faced the fact that I had a classic "poor me" personality, which remains stuck in difficult situations because of an unconscious fear of change, such as letting go of past hurts and an unwillingness to forgive and forget. This persona believes it's easier to complain and place blame than actually do something about a situation.

Finally, I became aware that my fear of letting go and the sympathy I sought manifested themselves in ill health: my body cried out because my creative spirit was in pain.

I learned to let go of the "poor me" syndrome by embracing two aspects of change: the outer expression of daily work and the inner perspective of self-awareness. In order to achieve balance and wholeness, I learned to cultivate an essential change in attitude.

During the process of self-discovery, my counselor and cherished friend advised me to consider looking at illness in a new way. "Don't make it wrong," she said, "it's like looking through a kaleidoscope: rotating it slightly allows one to see a whole new picture." I took her advice and gradually envisioned myself being completely healthy, vital, and successful—with a new, fulfilling career.

After my operation, my chiropractor and ayurvedic doctors advised me to alter my lifestyle, eat a healthy diet, and take daily, hour-long walks. I also attended several "wellness" lectures and was powerfully inspired by a guest speaker who had undergone two kidney transplants. He told us that he finally regained his health after he stopped looking back in fear. He said, "Remember, you can't go forward looking back!"

His advice really resonated with me. And in time, my determination to regain my health became stronger than my fear of changing my life's work. Consequently, I decided to learn a new profession: public relations and graphic design. Starting over wasn't easy and sometimes I felt totally inept, especially while taking intermediate Quark-Xpress classes at a local college. But I persevered, and my commitment to mastering new computer, business, and writing skills completely changed my life.

I have achieved a certain amount of success since then, although my journey hasn't been easy. And after much deliberation, I decided to relate the short version of my per-

Winter Maple. Oil, 20" × 24" © Timothy R. Thies, 2001.

sonal history that follows, as a way to further illustrate the importance of facing, embracing, and erasing the "poor me" state of mind.

In 1998, my family and I left the west and moved to Vermont. Northeast winters were long and sometimes bitter cold—to keep my spirit glowing, I'd sit near the wood-burning stove and reminisce. I hated going outside in zero-degree weather, and the snowy days evoked memories of happier winters: memories of my early childhood that seemed to wrap around me like my grandmother's warm woolen shawl. I'd recall the delicious smell of homemade bread baking in her huge, old-fashioned oven while we listened to my grandfather's stories.

My grandparents taught me to value honesty and integrity, and to pursue excellence. Though I lived with them only for a couple of years, their loving kindness nurtures me to this day. For example, even when I'm rushed, I still follow their wise councel: "Anything worth doing at all is worth doing well."

Prior to this time, my so-called normal life had changed dramatically when my father died in an airplane crash before my third birthday. My mother, who was a big-band singer, was forced to support me on her own, and had to travel with the band for weekend engagements. Frightened and somewhat naïve, she hired and fired several nannies to care for me. Then, after some friends tried to manipulate her into allowing them to adopt me, she took me back to Utah to live with her parents.

Unfortunately, the sweet time with my grandparents came to an end because my grandmother's heart condition forced them to leave me with a stepdaughter who was secretly jealous of my mother's success—somewhat resembling the tale of Cinderella and her stepsisters. I don't want to bore you with the whole long story, I just feel compelled to make the point that each of us has sad stories that keep us bound to the past.

Photograph of the author's parents, First Lieutenant and Mrs. Russell C. Williams

In time, the thought-patterns from this past continue, and somehow—by osmosis or some other means—we unconsciously take on a "poor me" persona. And before we realize it, we actually believe this state is our true lot in life. Unknowingly, we continue to relate our sad stories because we think we'll receive attention, and believe that sympathy from others will help alleviate the problem or diminish our sorrow. However, I believe this kind of experience is akin to peering through a window while a family sits down to a big turkey dinner: it looks delicious, but we never experience the real taste of Thanksgiving!

The most famous "starving artist" is undoubtedly Vincent Van Gogh. Clearly ahead of his time, the great nineteenth-century Impressionist suffered from mental and emotional torment due in part to his illness, a type of epilepsy that took the form of delusions and angry emotional behavior, and was compounded by his practice of drinking absinthe (72-proof alcohol).

As the worn-out story goes, Vincent was hopelessly distraught because he never sold a painting during his life and depended on his brother Theo to support his artistic career. I wonder how many people living today have actually seen an original Van

Gogh oil. But if you asked anyone on the street about him, I wager they would say, "Oh yeah, he's the artist who cut off his ear." Today, neurologists believe that Van Gogh suffered from a condition known as trigeminal neuralgia, and cut off his ear lobe to stop the pain.

Interestingly, during our trip to Auvers-sur-Oise, north of Paris, I uncovered a little-known fact while viewing a short film at La Maison de Van Gogh. Despite his illness, Vincent loved life and art passionately. Van Gogh always believed in the magnificence of human life; even his dreadful personal problems didn't make him lose his faith in the dignity of work. The painter Paul Signac, who knew Vincent well, thought that his painting companion personified charm and was ardent and good. Even though Vincent suffered from mental and physical imbalances, he was totally absorbed and inspired by the colors and beauty of the French countryside. He wrote his brother Theo and sister-in-law Jo, "Nature is very, very beautiful here," and hoped that his canvases would convey, "what I cannot say in words — the health and restorative forces that I see in the country."[2] During the last few months of his life, Vincent painted more than thirty canvases inspired by the cottages and the local landscape of the "real country," as he called it: the rural village of Auvers-sur-Oise.

It is my observation that when one lives in poverty and faces the constant struggle of daily life, it is nearly impossible to create one good painting, let alone thirty. The truth is that Theo supported his brother's artistic career because he believed in his work. It's also true that his peers recognized Vincent's work. In a letter dated April 23, 1890, Theo wrote his brother, "Your pictures at the Independents exhibition are having a lot of success." Theo also remarked that "Diaz stopped me in the street and said, 'Give your brother my compliments and tell him that his pictures are highly remarkable. Monet said that your pictures were the best of all in the exhibition. A lot of other artists have spoken to me about them. Serret came to our house to see the pictures, and he was enraptured."[3]

Since Theo and Vincent's correspondence was saved for posterity, I've often wondered why the screenwriters didn't relate the entire story while writing the film version of Van Gogh's life. Instead of focusing on Vincent's innovative artistic skills and creativity, they chose to emphasize his neurosis. It seems that filmmakers tend to focus on illness, alcohol and drug dependency when portraying the stories of artist's or musicians lives. No doubt this partial portrayal of Vincent's life (complicated by poverty and mental illness) has gradually become synonymous with the lives of many famous artists — so much so, that some aspiring painters are discouraged and warned by their

Sunflowers and Vintage Port. Oil, 20" × 30" © Timothy R. Thies, 2005. "Vincent Van Gogh painted many pictures of sunflowers because he believed they symbolize the power and beneficence of life. I painted these flowers because I love the color harmony of autumn." —TIMOTHY R. THIES

families not to even try. Timothy's relatives thought he was a bit "touched" when he gave up his advertising agency to pursue a career in fine art twenty-five years ago. But they're proud of his success and accomplishments now.

Another example of this deep-rooted belief in the starving-artist syndrome surfaced when a family visited our Vermont gallery to view Richard Schmid's paintings. Apparently, the son had tried to convince his parents to support his study of representational painting instead of paying for a traditional college education. The father was clearly angry and unwilling to contribute to an artist's life—a life he firmly believed was destined for failure. Even though the parents really wanted to understand their son's request, the conflict was quite apparent. They asked me many questions about the art world, and then I watched their attitudes soften a bit as they walked around the gallery. At the time, several of Schmid's captivating oils were on exhibit, along with *Zorro the Cat* by Nancy Guzik and *Dappled Light* by Timothy Thies. And each member of the family seemed to experience their exceptional beauty.

I sold many oil paintings during that show and a red sticker indicated each sale. Perhaps it was something I said, or—more likely—the sales (ranging from $1,200 to $10,000 for works by Guzik and Thies and from $30,000 to $60,000 for the Schmid pieces) changed their opinions. All I know is that the parents left the gallery feeling much more peaceful about their son's decision to study representational painting and become a professional artist.

My aim in sharing these true stories is to help cultivate a new perspective: I believe the time has come for artists to release old, debilitating thought patterns. And one way to accomplish this is to go on, despite the inevitable setbacks that arise in all creative fields of endeavor. When in doubt, I remind myself that there's always room for one more accomplished artist, writer, or even gallery owner!

I've also learned the importance of adopting a professional work ethic and a business-like attitude. Earning a living in the arts is a *business*. All businesses have their difficulties, and achieving success in any creative field is not easy. It takes years of disciplined work, but striving for the goal and reaching it is part of the joy.

It's even worth experiencing the darkness that leads to a new sense of self-discovery. An analogy might go something like this: when the earth is ravaged by drought, causing severe cracks in the soil, seeds that have been dormant for years finally germinate when rainfall again replenishes the soil. Darkness is one aspect of nature and so is the light of day. Therefore, I agree with Martin Luther King Jr.'s encouraging words and resolve not to fear the darkness. Besides, gazing at the stars on a moonless night is truly awesome!

P.S. I can almost hear you sigh, "As much as I don't want to admit it, this 'poor me' story sounds a bit like me. OK. Now what?"

I respond, "Well, if you're willing to move forward, read on. Part II is filled with advice and art resources. I borrowed some words of wisdom from Richard Schmid, George Carlson, as well as from luminaries like Sir Winston Churchill, and Robert Henri. The rest is taken directly from Timothy's and my life's journal of experiences.

LEFT: *Zorro the Cat.* Oil, 50" × 24" © Nancy Guzik, 1999.
ABOVE: *Dappled Light.* Oil, 30" × 24" © Timothy R. Thies, 1999.

NOTES

1. Martin Luther King, Jr., *The Words of Martin Luther King, Jr.: Selected by Coretta Scott King* (New York: New Market Press, 1987), 24 and 25.

2. Vincent Van Gogh, *The Complete Letters of Vincent Van Gogh vol. 3* (New York: Bullfinch Press, 2000), Letter 649, p. 295.

3. Theo Van Gogh, *The Complete Letters of Vincent Van Gogh, vol. 3* (New York: Bullfinch Press, 2000), Letter T 32, p. 568.

Portmagee Farm. Oil, 8" × 16" © Richard Schmid, 1994.

5
Cloudy-Day Wisdom

If aught I have said is truth, that truth shall reveal itself
In a clearer voice, and in words more kin to your own thoughts.

I go with the wind, but not down into emptiness;
And if this day is not a fulfillment of your needs and my love,
Then let it be a promise 'til another day.[1]

—KAHLIL GIBRAN

To MY WAY OF THINKING, ART IS AN ANALOGY FOR LIFE, and the duality of life is apparent in all of nature. Similarly, a masterwork on a sunny day is comprised of warm light and cool shadows. The lightest light, when placed next to the darkest dark, imparts depth as well as drama, and the hardest edge sets the stage for defining moments of exquisite beauty. Even when the day is overcast and the landscape is filled with subtle shadows, one can still find beauty in the soft and lost edges. Likewise, when clouds of doubt block the sunnier side of our being, it is helpful to delve a little deeper to experience the positive aspects of inner tranquility.

Wisdom unfolds a day at a time. I am still learning that the wise choice is to dream one's dream without fear of failure—and more importantly, without fear of success. I am just beginning to grasp the value of acceptance. We may never attain the full reality of our vision, and if we ever do, it may be years from now. Nevertheless, I believe time cannot destroy the fulfillment of pure creativity—time simply mellows and enhances its bouquet, as it does with fine wine.

The essential ingredients for achieving fulfillment in the arts are: keep striving, keep seeking knowledge, and remain vigilant. Shakespeare said, "Flowers are slow and weeds make haste." He also wrote, "Thoughts are but dreams till their effects are tried." And here's some advice from Thoreau to keep in mind when obstacles get in your way: "Go confidently in the direction of your dreams." If we are to help achieve a more

---

1. From *The Prophet* by Kahlil Gibran, copyright 1923 by Kahlil Gibran and renewed 1951 by Administrators C.T.A. of Kahlil Gibran Estate and Mary G. Gibran. Used by Permission of Alfred A. Knopf, a division of Random House, Inc.

Janice. Oil, 30" × 20" © Nancy Guzik, 2005.

"*Janice* is the first in a series of three paintings. It represents a journey of inner tranquility, yet it will speak individually to all who view it." —NANCY GUZIK

Montana Hollyhocks.
Oil, 30" × 40"
© Timothy R. Thies,
2004.

more peaceful world—a twenty-first-century world where fine art is revered and appreciated—then we, too, must never stop pursuing our dreams.

I want to leave you with a poem by Sir Alfred Lord Tennyson, the great poet laureate of England during Queen Victoria's reign. After the death of his closest friend, Arthur Hallum, Tennyson wrote these lines of hope, though he was experiencing great sorrow:

> Come, my friends.
> 'Tis not too late to seek a newer world.
> Tho' much is taken, much abides; that which we are we are,
> One equal temper of heroic hearts,
> Made weak by time and fate, but strong in will.
> To strive, to seek, to find and not to yield. [2]

Even during my darkest hours, his words never fail to encourage me. So, whenever you experience rejection, sorrow, fear, or doubt, try reading Tennyson's words of hope and courage.

Finally, please remember that it *is* possible for dreams to come true. It just takes time, perseverance, and a wealth of wisdom. I wish you grace and joy on your journey.

NOTES

1. From *The Prophet* by Kahlil Gibran, copyright 1923 by Kahlil Gibran and renewed 1951 by Administrators C.T.A. of Kahlil Gibran Estate and Mary G. Gibran. Used by Permission of Alfred A. Knopf, a division of Random House, Inc.

2. Sir Alfred Lord Tennyson: Excerpts from the poem "Ulysses," written in 1842.

Sunday Afternoon. Oil, 12" × 20" © Richard Schmid, 2003. ▶

WISDOM & THE DREAMER
Achieving Fulfillment in the Arts

PART II

"There are moments in our lives; there are moments in a day, when we seem to see beyond the usual. Such are the moments of our greatest happiness. Such are the moments of our greatest wisdom. If one could but recall his vision as some sort of sign. It was in this hope that the arts were invented. Sign-posts on the way to what may be. Sign-posts toward greater knowledge.[1]

— ROBERT HENRI

Poppies in Provence. Oil, 20" × 24" © Timothy R. Thies.

6
Tools for Achieving Fulfillment

AND YES, EVEN SUCCESS IN THE ARTS

Genius is eternal patience.
—MICHELANGELO

*M*AKING THE TRANSITION FROM amateur to professional, full-time artist is one of the most difficult passages one can make. Before you embark on your own career in fine art, I urge you to explore some or all of these tools. Though Timothy and I were born with determination and the entrepreneurial spirit, I devised these steps to help guide us through the many twists and turns we faced.

Unfortunately, there are no guarantees for earning a living as a painter, sculptor, portrait painter, or author, etc. However, if becoming a professional artist is your all-consuming passion—as it was for Timothy, this advice will serve a definite purpose. It will help you develop new skills and it will provide you with a plan of action. If you're feeling a bit overwhelmed, believe me, I can relate. Writing my first book is quite an undertaking and I constantly remind myself to simply complete one page at a time. Even if you begin with small steps, please keep going. Fully embrace the idea of succeeding.

❧ INTROSPECTION

1. Spend some quality time alone and write down your realistic objectives. What are your financial goals?
2. What are your artistic goals? List the advantages for becoming a professional artist.
3. What is your purpose? Draft a personal mission statement.
   Example:
   "Art chose me. Being an artist is a passionate pursuit of something indefinable and indescribable, it is a driving inner force to paint. Fine art is my life's work."
   —TIMOTHY R. THIES

Having done this, it is my belief that you will remain steadfast to your goals even if times get tough.

❀ TAKE ACTION: Adopt what I call the Four **P**'s

4. **Practice**: Never stop perfecting your artistic skills.
5. **Perseverance**: Continue entering shows even if your work is rejected.
6. **Patience**: Realize that being an artist is your life's work! Learn to enjoy the journey even if it takes years to achieve success.
7. **Professionalism**: This is one of the most significant marketing skills to master.
   a. Never underestimate the importance of your image—your personal appearance and your promotional materials.
   b. Always use good manners. No one wants to be around someone who wastes his or her time and complains a lot.
   c. Remain respectful of the artists who already are recognized by galleries and art collectors.
   d. Keep your word. Do what you say you're going to do. Honesty and integrity do count.

❀ MARKETING: How to do it with a small budget

8. Master the Art of Mini-Market Research.
9. Take a business trip and visit the galleries personally and that may be a good fit for your work.
   Do not bring in your paintings or slides unless invited by the gallery director. Please dress well; it always makes a good first impression. It's amazing, but sales people respond to clientele that are well groomed. So do gallery owners, directors and the ever-important collectors. Visiting galleries provides the perfect chance to check out the gallery personnel. Do they ignore you or are they friendly as you enter the gallery?
10. Observe other artist's paintings.
    a. Check out the quality of their professional framing. Are the paintings presented in 22-karat custom gold leaf moldings? On the other hand, are they made of hardwood? Or are less expensive metal-leaf frames with the chopped corners used through out the gallery?
    b. Take note of the painting styles. Are they representational or abstract, or are they art prints—lithographs under glass or giclee' printed on canvas?

c. Very discreetly, note the sizes, prices, and the quality of the framing on the featured paintings.

11. If you would like the gallery to consider your work, ask for the owner's business card, introduce yourself and find out when the director will review new work. Then, say thanks and make a timely exit! Please show respect for his or her busy schedule.

❧ MARKETING TOOLS

12. When you return from your trip, write a thank you note and let the gallery director know you'll be sending them a packet of information the week they'll be reviewing work. Most likely, the gallery is not accepting new artists, but it is worth preparing your promotional materials anyway. If your work is truly good, it will be remembered!

13. Prepare your promotional packet. To make it look distinctive, hire a graphic designer. If you can't afford to work with an expert, learn to do it yourself, like I did. This is easier and less costly in the end, especially when its time to up-date your resumé, etc. If you choose this route, I highly recommend learning Microsoft Word, Quark Xpress, or In-Design, a new software program. Alternatively, if you prefer to work with a designer, *Writers Market* will give you an idea of what to pay a professional writer/desktop designer. It may cost you a bit up-front, but a well-designed set of clear and concise documents will make a great first impression. And it will set you apart from other artists.

    Please include the following:
    a. Your up-to-date resumé. Include gallery representation, exhibitions, your education, and affiliations if any.
    b. Your one page Biography. Highlight your achievements, awards, etc. and include a brief account of your artistic background. If you write this yourself, always check your spelling and hire an editor to correct grammatical mistakes.
    c. A sampling of your work: (slides are costly and tend to be misplaced). Send along a few color photos of your best works placed inside clear plastic sheet protectors, available at any office supply store. I usually mount one or two images of paintings on white paper before I place them in the sheet protectors.
    d. A list of titles, medium, sizes, and retail prices. Use the unframed size of the piece—height first, then width. Retail prices include the cost of the frame. Most collectors want to know the date of the work as well.

e. Put the whole packet together in a good quality 3-ring folder and always include a cover letter and your business card. If you want it returned, please send along a self addressed stamped envelope or SASE.

f. Send slides *only* when invited by the gallery owner or director. It is quite easy to lose track of unsolicited slides in a busy gallery.

14. Take note of other artist's website pages, do research first, and then decide if having a presence on the Internet is right for you. Websites are wonderful but only work well when the web address is included in a magazine advertising the artist's work. Ads are costly and so is a website if collectors are not aware yours exists. Beautiful or compelling work drives a collector to browse a site, so don't waste your money on bogus sites that promise you the moon.

❀ ADVICE ON FRAMING

15. Use professional framing. If you can't afford it, learn to do it yourself. That is exactly what Timothy did and in the process, he mastered the art of 23-karat gold leaf framing. Fine art collectors recognize good quality. A great looking frame is very much like icing on the cake!

16. For excellent frame resources, buy a copy of *Picture Framing Magazine.* Then make a choice. Does your work look best with finished corners (custom frames have finished corners) or chopped corners? This is the kind of framing done by most local frame stores.

17. Custom gold leaf frames are made-to-order. For example, a 22-karat gold leaf Florentine style molding from a frame maker is a work of art in and of itself. Frame shops often charge the same amount for a metal leaf frame and are more commercial looking.

18. Always secure the wiring on the back of each frame and make sure the wire does not show past the top of the frame when your painting hangs on the wall. Don't forget to sign your work before shipping them to a gallery or a show. It is quite helpful to clearly write the title, medium, and size on the back along with your name.

Example: *Title,* medium, size, © your name, year. It is also extremely helpful to number your work.

19. Take a workshop on the fine art of framing especially if it becomes too costly for you to buy them from a frame shop.

1. Write down your goals. Review them and set new attainable objectives each month. Then write your long-range goals in quarterly, yearly, and five-year increments. Goals are like a road map leading you in the direction of your dreams.
2. Write down your purpose as an artist.
3. Spend quality time doing market research. Remember, your art is also a product and must be realistically priced.
4. Design professional looking marketing materials.
5. Use great framing to compliment your art.
6. Take an objective look at your own work. Ask fellow artists or teachers for a critique and be *willing to listen* to make improvements. It's wise to leave your ego at the door, by the way.
7. Be determined to succeed!
8. Ask yourself: what am I willing to do so I will not fail?
9. Realize there are many sacrifices an artist must make. Ask yourself: what am I willing to give up?
10. If your answer is yes, adopt a new motto. Ours is: Failure is not an option!
11. Don't give up on your dream. Take Sir Winston Churchill's advice. He said, "Never flinch, never weary, never despair."

❀ MOST IMPORTANTLY, realize that the journey is just as important as reaching the goal!

The English Gardener. Oil, 14" × 11" © Timothy R. Thies.

7
Collectors and the Unspoken Language of Art

If the viewer experiences art in the same inspired state as the artist,
Then the observer will also comprehend why we create works of art.
—TIMOTHY R. THIES

AT SOME TIME IN THEIR CAREER, all artists ask why collectors buy the paintings they do—a question that is usually followed by, "How can I entice them to buy more of mine?" To help you understand what attracts fine-art collectors to the work of certain living artists while that of others goes unnoticed, I asked several prominent connoisseurs about their reasons for collecting. Although several acquire art as an investment, their answers were as varied as the representational paintings and sculpture they own, but they did have a common theme: an emotional connection with the work they purchase. Interestingly, some collectors agreed with Leonardo da Vinci's concept of *cosa mentali,* the spiritual component that makes fine art more than just the application of paint to a surface.

When in the presence of a beautiful nature setting, it is easy to produce a mood of peace and joy at being a small part of this sublime creation. The art I choose to collect is based on the mood it produces in me. I use art to return me to that joyful state of being where I am reminded of my connection to the Divine. — *C. B.*

My soul was moved when I first saw *The English Gardener* [by Timothy Thies]. It was as if my father, whom this painting resembled—same build, same gestures— was there in front of me! He loved his greenhouse as much as life itself. Two years prior he passed away from Alzheimer's disease. However, this painting allows me to imagine his presence. The gardener also reminded me of my husband's father, Pop-Pop, as our children called him, who spent endless hours in our greenhouse tending the geraniums. Two weeks before I first saw this painting, he had joined my father in God's Kingdom. There are many reasons the soul is led to purchase art. I feel the moment art moves you relates to the moment the artist had in mind when he or she set out to capture the scene. This is the silent whisper that comes to both the artist and the collector—uniting them in a special way. —*J. S.*

Sacred Pines. Oil, 30" × 18" © Timothy R. Thies.

Sometimes a painting stirs strong memories, transporting us into a favorite time or place long past. For example, upon acquiring a forest landscape one collector reminisced:

> As a child, I loved the forest. Our house in the suburbs of Maryland, bordered by acres and acres of forestland, backed up to a reservoir. My twin sister, our two brothers and I spent countless hours back in the woods. We used to peel up pieces of moss, move it to one spot, and make little beds and sleep back in the woods on it (scared the whole time!). This painting reminds me of our marvelous childhood! —S. L.

Then there are art collectors who purchase paintings for the pure joy of viewing them and the ambience of peace they create:

> One can't help but look at something beautiful. There is an elegance and beauty in art that's so touching; it illuminates and enlivens the beauty within me. — V. F.

> Most artists tell you that they paint because they have to—it is a calling. Collecting art is much the same for the collector—it too is a calling. We cannot imagine our walls without art. Art is life, the expression of all that we love about life. Everyday we enjoy the beauty of a rose, a fox trotting over stones in a stream, the glow of the sun on the lower falls of the Yellowstone river, or a small child reading a book. We chose the paintings in our collection for our continuous enjoyment of all the things we love about life. —C. B. McC.

> All of the art I collect evokes emotions of peace, joy, and contentment. Like music, I feel I need art in my home to help create an atmosphere of beauty that gives me a deep sense of well-being. — V. B.

One collector shared a special vision for the future:

> My wife is purposefully, carefully and discerningly, putting together a collection of master works because it is an inspiration for her; and because she has a vision that such a collection will inspire others in the future. She has been, and is, very committed to this vision. — W. B.

Still other fine art connoisseurs, whose collections are replete with priceless masterpieces, purchase fine art for its beauty and as an investment. One such collector uses his business acumen to "secure stores of value for family assets." However, he explained that the main reason he and his wife collect representational paintings is "our

North Idaho Marsh.
Oil, 14" × 18"
© Timothy R. Thies.

dedication, among other things, to aiding in establishing a strong worldwide market for Realism painted by living artists."

In addition, several art patrons have told me they peruse web sites such as AskArt.com to help them determine the value of American paintings or sculpture sold at auction. According to AskART's American Art Index—a source of auction records for more than 32,000 American artists—prices paid for art by living artists have significantly increased from 1998–2005. In part, this increase may be attributed to worldwide admiration and nostalgia for art of the American West.

The artist and writer Don Gray wrote an essay titled "Masterpieces of the American West," on the Philip F. Anschutz Collection. It sheds some light on the popularity of collecting art with a Western theme. In it, Gray examines some "meanings of the West in reality and myth":

> The West is, and has been, a metaphor for freedom, danger, challenge, expectation and opportunity. It is, and has been, wide-open spaces; great mountains and canyons; a bigger, higher, more dramatic sky; a rougher, arid, more primitive way of life. But the West is not just a place, it's an idea, a feeling, the stuff of man's eternal dreams of quest and fulfillment.[1]

In addition, a couple shared their connection with the silent stories captured by the artist's brush or forged by the sculptor's hands:

46

A common thread runs through our collection of representational art. Whether it's a landscape, a portrait, or a still life, we are drawn to paintings that move you beyond the surface into the essence of the subject—paintings that give you the sense that something more is going on than what you see. The artist's interpretation and subtle variations in brushwork, color, and edges can give a painting an inner quality that draws you in and makes you feel that you're participating in the moment—making a connection with the subject and the artists. Giving you stories and memories, you can't quite know but want to imagine. The emotional connection is what we look for in a painting and why we collect original art. —*D. & M. B.*

With this in mind, it becomes even more apparent that art is an unspoken language—a direct communication between the artist and the viewer. Therefore, I recommend knowing to whom you are speaking, especially if your intention is to establish a market for your work.

Richard Schmid, one of the most prosperous American artists in history, is a master at this unspoken language, and his work has helped to establish a powerful force for the renaissance of representational art worldwide. In addition to excelling at communication between artist and viewer, however, he has much to say to other artists; when I asked him to provide some friendly professional advice, he spoke of the need for artists to realize that their paintings are products:

Once you finish a painting and you wish to sell it, I believe you must regard it as if it were a product, albeit a precious and special product—nonetheless a product to be marketed appropriately. There are many things required to sell it in order to receive the return it deserves. Granted you often must listen to the demands of gallery owners and other agents—you don't have to agree with them—but that's part of it. Remember that you are dealing with people who for the most part are business persons and their motives are centered on profit. Remember too that you are the creator of your art and as such should have final word on pricing your work. Your good name and reputation as an artist are always on the line when you are out in the public arena of the art world. These are some of the fundamental ideas you need to keep in mind when dealing with the reality of the art world.[2]

I then asked Richard to comment on the foundation of his own success and to share his views on the art world today from that perspective. He replied:

The great golden ages in art have always been times that celebrated the highest aspirations of the human spirit. We are however in a period in which the nihilistic aspects of human experience are emphasized and publicized. Now as we enter the twenty-first century, the demise of this unfortunate art trend is becoming increasingly apparent as more and more thoughtful artists express something that has meaning to it. I choose to paint what is meaningful to me, and if my work is compelling, it will be significant to someone else.[2]

Richard paints his view of the world. "Painting is a direct visual communication between the artist and the viewer. It is a joyous affirmation—a reverence for just being alive. It's a realization that being an artist is a privilege—it's a prayer to creation."[2]

Aspiring artists can learn much from George Carlson, who is undoubtedly one of the most successful American sculptors and painters of our time. His powerful work graces numerous private and public museum collections throughout the world and he is the recipient of the Prix de West, seven gold medals, and countless other awards. He says:

> The artistic act of producing something that is fine is mainly the act of caring, giving and loving. Success of a work is when the viewer feels the same wonder that drew you to the subject in the first place."[3]

If we learn only one thing by following the example of these two great masters, it is this: the success of their work is measured by their great love of the beauty and dignity of life. Carlson states it best: "When I am in the presence of the subject, I strive to be in sympathy with that life form, to use every ounce of my talent to forge a work that will honor that life."[3]

If you strive for excellence, and convey your own love or passion for your subjects—expressing your inspired state as you paint—you too can forge a powerful bond with fine art collectors.

NOTES

1. Don Gray, *Essay, Philip F. Anschutz Collection:* "Masterpieces of the American West," 1985. Copyrighted essay by Don Gray reprinted with permission.

2. Richard Schmid, conversations with Kristen Thies 2004-2006. Used by permission.

3. George Carlson, "The Year of the Horse: Bronzes & Drawings." Catalog (Billings, MT, Nicholas Fine Art) 2002. Quotes reprinted with permission of the artist. Photograph of Bronze sculpture, *Light of Dawn*, courtesy of George and Pamela Carlson. ©George Carlson 2003.

48

Light of Dawn. Bronze, 27½" H × 11" W × 10" D. Edition: 21. © George Carlson, 2003.

8
Important Art-Related Documents

I OFFER THE FOLLOWING OUTLINE to protect the gallery/artist relationship. It is important to be aware that a complete and appropriate agreement includes additional legal items and issues. This outline is intended only as a general guideline.

1. The date the agreement will begin and end, and the conditions for terminating on any basis other than the specified end-date. The ideal is a yearly contract that can either be renewed or re-negotiated, unless otherwise specified.

2. The responsibility of the artist to consign work to the gallery and the gallery's responsibilities in return, including all specifics (such as pricing arrangements, the gallery's role as non-exclusive agent for the artist's work, etc.). It is customary for the artist to set the price of their work; the gallery must ask the artist's permission to discount any work prior to closing the sale.

3. The amount of each party's commission upon sale of a work, the collection of taxes, agreement to ship work to customer only upon receipt of valid payment, and the timeframe in which the gallery shall notify the artist of a sale and forward the commission. (Example: Gallery shall pay the artist x-percentage sales commission and shall retain x-percentage. Ideally, this takes place within one to two weeks after the sale.)

4. It is customary for the artist to pay for crating and shipping to the gallery.

5. It is also customary for the gallery to pay for public relations and ads, or split the cost of ads with the artist. However, the gallery retains the right to choose the size and amount of advertisements. The works of new artists are rarely if ever advertised, but their name is usually listed in the gallery's roster of artists.

6. Generally, the gallery ships any unsold pieces back to the artist at its own expense.

7. The artist always retains the copyright.

8. The gallery is liable for loss or damage while the artist's work is on its premises, or during shipment to a customer or during return shipment to the artist. Conversely, it is the artist's responsibility to deliver the work to the gallery, profes-

sionally framed, in excellent condition, and by the promised date. It is also advisable to write the name of the painting on the back.

9. Artists are responsible for notifying the gallery about any inquiries they receive directly from potential collectors regarding their work if the gallery is advertising that work, either on the web or through print ads.

10. All official notices transmitted between the artist and the gallery shall be in writing and signed by the artist or the gallery owner.

11. This agreement, signed and dated, is the only agreement between the parties.

Remember that a sound agreement protects both parties, so it is a good idea to discuss these points with your dealer or gallery before you draft your document. The artist/gallery relationship is precious; therefore, I recommend presenting these eleven ideas with this goal in mind.

9
Artist's Guide to Resources

Upon the subject of education:
Not presuming to dictate any plan or system respecting it,
I can only say that I view it as the most important subject
Which we as a people may be engaged in.

— ABRAHAM LINCOLN

Recommended Reading
Fine Art Books: Painting Instruction

Richard Schmid, *Alla Prima: Everything I Know about Painting.* (New Hampshire: Stove Prairie Press, LLC, 1998).

David A. Leffel, *An Artist Teaches: Reflections on the Art of Painting.* (New Mexico: Bright Light Publishing, 2003).

Burton Silverman, *Painting People.* (New York: Watson Guptill, 1977).

John Howard Sanden, *The Portraits of John Howard Sanden.* (New York: Madison Square Press, 2001). Also by John Howard Sanden: *Painting the Head in Oil,* 1976.

Emile A. Gruppé and Charles Movalli, *Brushwork for the Oil Painter.* (New York: Watson Guptill, 1983).

Edgar Payne, *Composition of Outdoor Painting.* (Minnesota: Payne Studios, Inc., 1988).

John F. Carlson, *Carlson's Guide to Landscape Painting.* (New York: Dover Publications, 1958).

Ralph Mayer, *The Artist's Handbook of Materials and Techniques.* (New York: The Viking Press, 1970).

John H. Vanderpoel, *The Human Figure.* (New York: Dover Publications, 1958).

DVDs and Videos

The Captain's Portrait—An Afternoon of Painting With Richard Schmid. (New Hampshire: Stove Prairie Press, LLC, 2001). ©Richard Schmid 2001.

Richard Schmid Paints the Landscape: November. (New Hampshire: Stove Prairie Press, LLC, 2002). ©Richard Schmid 2002.

Richard Schmid Paints the Landscape: June. (New Hampshire: Stove Prairie Press, LLC, 2003). ©Richard Schmid 2003.

The Capital Collection: Number one in a series of Retrospective Works by Richard Schmid. (New Hampshire: Stove Prairie Press, LLC, 2006). ©Richard Schmid 2006.

Inspirational Art Books and Catalogs

John Asaro, *A New Romanticism.* (California: Artra Publishing, Inc., 1991).

Clyde Aspevig, *Exhibition Catalog 2004.* (Montana: Juniper Ridge Studios, 2004).

Clyde Aspevig, *Elemental Solitude: The Landscapes of Clyde Aspevig.* (NY: Rockwell Museum of Western Art and Montana: Juniper Ridge Studios, 2005).

George Carlson, *Dignity in Art.* (California: Gene Autry Western Heritage Museum, 1993).

George Carlson, *Year of the Horse: Bronzes & Drawings.* (Montana: Nicholas Fine Art, 2002).

Robert Henri, *The Art Spirit.* (CO: Westview Press, 1984).

Ned Jacob, *Sacred Paint.* (New Mexico: Fenn Galleries Publishing, Inc., 1979).

Sherrie McGraw, *The Language of Drawing.* (New Mexico: Bright Light Publishing, 2004).

Dean Mitchell, *The Early Years.* (Kansas: Mitchell Studios, 1996).

Dean Mitchell, *Beauty in the Real.* (Arizona: Mitchell Studios, 2004).

Burton Silverman: *Sight & Insight: The Art of Burton Silverman.* (New York: Madison Square Press, 1998). And, *The Intimate Eye: The Drawings of Burt Silverman.* (Salt Lake City: Brigham Young University Press, 2007.)

Richard Ormond: *John Singer Sargent Exhibition catalogue.* (NJ: Princeton University Press) Published in North America in 1998.

Richard Kendall: *VAN GOGH'S, Van Goghs: Masterpieces from the Van Gogh Museum.* (Washington, DC: National Gallery of Art, 1998).

Art Reference
Marketing and Career Books

Daniel Grant, *The Artist's Resource Handbook* (New York: Allworth Press, 1996).

Caroll Michels, *How To Survive and Prosper As An Artist: Selling Yourself Without Selling Your Soul.* (New York: Henry Holt and Company, 1992).

Writer's Digest Books, *Artist's & Graphic Designer's Market: Where & How to Sell Your Illustration, Fine Art, Graphic Design.* (Ohio: F&W Publications, 2000.) Please note that this book is published yearly. Do use the latest edition to insure that the information is current.

Tad Crawford, *Business and Legal Forms for Fine Artists.* (New York: Allworth Press, 1999). The book also includes forms on a CD. This is an excellent resource to refer to again and again. I highly recommend using the sample forms when drafting your own agreements—it is a simple and effective way to protect you and your work when dealing with artist's models, if you are asked to paint a commission piece, or when writing your artist gallery agreement.
1. Model Release Form.
2. Contract for a Commissioned Artwork.
3. Artist-Gallery Agreement with Gallery Statement of Account.

Publicity & Graphic Design

Robin Williams, *The Non Designer's Design Book: Design and Typographic Principles for the Visual Novice.* (California: Peachpit Press, A division of Addison-Wesley Publishing, CO. Copyright ©Robin Williams, 1994).

Susan Abbott and Barbara Webb, *Fine Art Publicity: The Complete Guide For Galleries & Artists.* (CT: The Art Business News Library, 1991).

Books on Creativity, Success, and Wisdom

Julia Cameron, *The Artist's Way.* (New York: Jeremy P. Tarcher /Putnam1992 & 2002.) Copyright ©Julia Cameron, 2002.

Chérie Carter-Scott, PH.D. *If Success Is A Game, These Are The Rules.* (New York: Broadway Books 2000.) Copyright © Chérie Carter-Scott, PH.D 2000.

Helen Exley, *. . . And Wisdom Comes Quietly.* (MA: Exley Publications, LTD, 2000). Selection and arrangement Copyright ©Helen Exley 2000.

Dr. Wayne W. Dyer, *Inspiration: Your Ultimate Calling.* (CA: Hay House 2006). Copyright ©Dr. Wayne W. Dyer, 2006.

Peonies and Laurel Leaves. Oil, 8" × 16" © Richard Schmid.

Kristen Thies, true to herself and to all others, and empowered by actual, deep belief in the power and possibility of life dreams, is like a great painting's canvas: behind the scene, easily overlooked or forgotten—but the sure and solid foundation upon which the best things in the Art World—and in life—are built.

— PAUL SODERBERG

Kristen Thies *and* the Foundation of the Art World

KRISTEN THIES BELIEVES IN the power of inspiration just as Michelangelo did when he wrote, "The true work of art is but a shadow of the divine perfection." She explains her lifetime love of art this way, "It's like a golden thread of knowledge—fine art connects us to the great artists of past ages whose works have long endured."

The secret to Kristen's remarkable success as a gallery owner, graphic designer, publisher, executive producer, and publicist is that conviction, Michelangelo's certainty, that there are higher standards by which we can measure our own creativity. Leading artists today believe we are on the threshold of a great rebirth of art. The rebirth must begin by rediscovering and renewing the forgotten standards of the past–such as Plato's ancient trinity of beauty, truth and goodness.

One of the eternal verities, as true today as it was in Michelangelo's day, is that works of art have the power to speak directly to the human soul, and thereby to enrich and uplift. The paintings by the three artists to whom Kristen has long dedicated her incredible instincts and amazing skills all express that verity: paintings by Richard Schmid, Nancy Guzik and Timothy R. Thies are never objects, always conduits of that power, which then touches the viewer's soul.

No one becomes as influential and profoundly supportive of true greatness by accident. So the fascinating question about Kristen Thies is: What made her that way? And the answer is: Dreams did. Rather, her unshakable belief in life dreams and in dreams coming true, is what made her so truly remarkable.

And rare. It takes all kinds of people to make the Art World go 'round, and it sometimes seems that this strange and wonderful little world's spin is controlled by men and women motivated by the base emotions, including greed, envy, jealousy, deception, and nonsense. But it also takes the rarest kind of individual in Art, and this is the woman or man who truly believes in the higher emotions, like beauty, honesty, altruism, and truth. It was this kind of rare individual, the Kristen kind of person, whom Shakespeare was describing when he had Polonius say in *Hamlet,* "This above all: to thine ownself be true, /And it must follow, as the night the day, /Thou canst not then be false to any man."

The Color Wizardry of Timothy R. Thies

PAUL SODERBERG

*T*IMOTHY R. THIES is one of America's finest living artists because he understands that the best things in life are all invisible.

Laughter, love, wind, the spirit, life itself—all are visible only through the things they animate. Thies's paintings somehow capture not just visible objects but also the invisible vital forces that animate them. Looking at his paintings of trees, you can hear the breeze moving through their branches. Looking at his portraits, you see not just a face but a living, breathing unique personality. His still lifes are more life than still. Left outdoors, his Florals would attract nectar-seeking butterflies. Through his seascapes you feel the pull of the tide. It is these aspects of Timothy's paintings that perform a sort of magic: you, the viewer, are drawn into each scene, ceasing to be a passive observer and becoming an active participant.

This wizardry with paint is the result of Timothy R. Thies's many years of study, practice, experimentation, and above all observation. "The key to painting anything is observation," he says. "Another helpful hint is to relax, because if you're all tensed up about what you're looking at, or about what you're going to paint, then nothing will come out right." He follows his own advice: "Relaxed and open, I sink slowly into the rhythm of Nature as my painting unfolds with each stroke of my brush."

Always seeking new natural vistas, and fond of adventure, Thies in 1973 traveled west from Iowa, and was awestruck by the majesty of the Rocky Mountains. It was during this trip that he decided to make Denver his home and to attend the Colorado Institute of Art. Thereafter he traveled widely throughout America and Europe, and he studied at The National Academy Museum and School of Fine Art in New York with one of America's greatest 20th-Century painters, Nelson Shanks. Timothy also has taken workshops with Clyde Aspevig, Len Chmiel, and David Leffel, and at the Loveland Academy of Art, he studied anatomy and sculpting with Jon Zahourek. Timothy has also been mentored by Richard Schmid, another of America's greatest 20th-Century painters, since 1996. In addition, since 2000, Thies has been a member of The Village Arts of Putney, in Southern Vermont—the painting group founded by Nancy Guzik and Richard Schmid. In turn, Timothy has taught at several prestigious art schools, including the Scottsdale Artists' School in Arizona and has conducted numerous painting workshops in Vermont, Massachusetts, Florida, Alabama, and north Idaho.

All he learned from those many accomplished artists and in those prestigious institutions, coupled with his own natural instincts for observing and sensing the "heart and soul" of any scene, explains the artistic mastery for which Timothy R. Thies is becoming famous nationwide. That in turn explains why his paintings have won so many awards throughout America, including the Best of Show Award at The Bennington Center for the Arts in 2002 and, more recently, in 2005, two awards in the top one hundred paintings of the Landscape Category selected by the International Art Renewal Center's 2nd Annual Salon Competition. In addition, Timothy was invited to become a faculty member of the Portrait Society of America in 2006 and serves as the P.S.A.'s Co-Ambassador for the State of Idaho.

Paintings by Timothy R. Thies have also been exhibited in many of America's most prestigious annual exhibitions, including the Northwest Rendezvous Exhibition, The Colorado Governor's Invitational, The American Society of Portrait Artist's competition held at the Metropolitan Museum of Art, The Boston International Fine Arts Show, The Copley Society of Boston, and the National Arts Club in New York. His paintings may also be seen in Coeur d'Alene, Idaho, in annual shows at West Wind Fine Art, the gallery he and his wife Kristen founded.

All this exposure and recognition, and his increasing circle of collectors, has not altered Timothy's essential values, nor diluted the freshness and intensity he brings to each new canvas. To view one of his magical paintings is not simply to become a participant in the scene, but also to witness a work created by a rare fine artist who understands the importance of reverence for life—especially life's invisible things.

Timothy R. Thies in his north Idaho studio.

Richard Schmid Biography

RICHARD SCHMID was born in Chicago, Illinois in 1934. His earliest artistic influence came from his maternal grandfather, Julian Oates, an architectural sculptor. Richard's initial studies in landscape painting, figure drawing, and anatomy began at the age of twelve and continued into Classical techniques under William H. Mosby at the American Academy of Art in Chicago.

Mosby, a graduate of the Belgian Royal Academy in Brussels and the Superior Institute in Antwerp, was a technical expert on European and American realism. Studies with him involved working exclusively from life, at first using the conceptual and technical methods of the Flemish, Dutch, and Spanish masters, and eventually the late 19th century Italian, French, Slavic, Scandinavian, and American painters. The emphasis in all periods was on Alla Prima, or Direct Painting systems of the various periods. However, Richard's individual style and the content of his work developed along personal lines.

At ceremonies hosted by the American Society of Portrait Artists in the Grace Rainey Rogers Auditorium in the Metropolitan Museum of Art in 2000, Richard Schmid received the John Singer Sargent Medal for Lifetime Achievement. Richard Ormond, Sargent's grandnephew, presented the award. In 2005, the Portrait Society of America presented him with the Gold Medal Award at their Portrait Conference held in Washington, DC. In addition Richard was presented with an honorary Doctorate Degree in Fine Arts from the Lyme Academy College of Fine Arts in 2004.

Throughout his career, Richard Schmid has promoted art education through his books, articles, workshops, seminars, and television presentations. He travels widely in the Western Hemisphere for his subjects, and currently lives in New Hampshire with his wife, the painter Nancy Guzik.

Richard Schmid and Nancy Guzik in New York City. © West Wind Fine Art, 2002. ▶

Selected Group Exhibitions

The Butler Institute of American Art, Youngstown, OH

The Smithsonian Institution, Washington, D.C.

The Pennsylvania Academy of Fine Arts, Philadelphia, P

The Art Institute of Chicago, Chicago, IL

The Connecticut Academy of Fine Arts, Hartford, CT

Beijing Exhibition Center, Peoples Republic of China, Beijing, China

The American Watercolor Society, New York, NY

The Thomas Gilcrease Museum of American Art, Tulsa, OK

The Frye Museum, Seattle, WA

The Palette and Chisel Academy of Fine Arts, Chicago, IL

The Colorado Historical Society, Denver, CO

Project Hope Exhibitions, Williamsport, PA

The Loveland Museum, Loveland, CO

The Bennington Center For Art & Culture, Bennington, VT

The Harvard Club of Boston, Boston, MA

Nancy Guzik Biography

$\mathcal{F}$OR THE PAST NINETEEN YEARS, Nancy Guzik has been quietly perfecting not only her skills, but the focus of her work, and the result, in one critic's words, is something like Joy. She brings to the world of Art a warmth unseen in painting for generations. Rarely has Art come to us from so pure a spirit. Her underlying themes are always of faith, trust, and love.

Nancy Guzik attended The American Academy of Art in Chicago and The Lyme Academy College of Fine Art in Old Lyme, Connecticut. However, it was her close association and ensuing relationship with Richard Schmid that brought her painting to its full potential. Nancy and Richard married in April of 1998.

She is the recipient of many awards including the Grand Prize from International Artist Magazine for her Floral still life, "Openings," three Gold Medals from the Palette & Chisel Academy in Chicago and the First prize Award from the Midwest Pastel Society. Her work has been featured in *International Artist Magazine*, *Art of the West*, *Art Talk*, and *Southwest Art Magazine*. She is the director of the Putney Painters, the group she and Richard Schmid founded in southern Vermont.

For the past ten years, Guzik's paintings have been exhibited in the Richard Schmid Art Auction, in Colorado, West Wind Fine Art Gallery exhibitions in Vermont and Coeur d'Alene, Idaho (since 1998). She has also been invited to participate in The Governor's Invitational Show, in Colorado; The Settler's West Invitational in Tucson, AZ; The Boston International Fine Art Show; The Harvard Club of Boston; The Salon d'Artes in Denver, CO; and The Manchester Invitational Exhibition in Vermont. Her work has also been exhibited at the Palette & Chisel Academy, in Chicago; The Southern Vermont Arts Center, in Manchester, Vermont; The Hollister Corporation; and The Bennington Center for the Arts and The Village Arts of Putney in Vermont.

◀ *Openings*. Oil, 36" × 24" © Nancy Guzik.

Timothy and Rudy (*Rudy is on the left.*)

Images of Richard Schmid's and Nancy Guzik's paintings were acquired
with the assistance of the artists and West Wind Fine Art Gallery,
Coeur d'Alene, Idaho. Photographic Processing by Advantage
Color, Hayden, Idaho. Design and Production by Stephen
Stinehour, Lunenburg, Vermont. Ordering information:
Cornerstone Fulfillment Service, Bondville, Vermont.
802- 297-3771, cornerstoneorders@adelphia.net
To view paintings by Richard Schmid, Nancy
Guzik, and Timothy R. Thies, please visit
www.WestWindFineArt.com,
208-765-3878.

DISCLAIMER

The information in *Wisdom and the Dreamer: Achieving Fulfillment in the Arts*, is the opinion of the author and the publisher, West Wind Fine Art, LLC, and is presented for informational purposes only. The information does not provide any guarantees that individual readers will become successful artists, earn income from their work, or become nationally known in the field of fine art.

The information presented is not meant to replace the advice of legal, financial, or other professional counsel. Individuals should consult an attorney, accountant, and additional art consultants and publicists for specific applications to their individual fine art ventures. Individuals should always gather and consider more than one source of information in order to make well-informed decisions.

West Wind Fine Art specializes in traditional, representational fine art of a conservative nature. This may include original paintings, limited edition lithographs and giclee' art prints—a new digital process for printing fine art prints.

West Wind Fine Art, LLC reserves the right to represent work by traditional, representational artists. Therefore, West Wind Fine Art reserves the right to decline representation of any artist's work that is not within our specialty.

West Wind Fine Art, LLC is under no contractual obligation to provide free goods or services of any kind to anyone for any reason at any time.

The resource guide in Part II of *Wisdom and the Dreamer: Achieving Fulfillment in the Arts,* is the opinion of the author and the publisher, West Wind Fine Art, LLC, and is presented for informational purposes only. The author and publisher acknowledge that there are many other expert art publications, books, and DVDs on the market. However, these resources are included because the author and publisher have direct experience and knowledge of their publications, products, and services. West Wind Fine Art, LLC, has received written permission to include these company names in the resource guide. West Wind Fine Art, LLC, is not an owner, partner, or business venturer with any of the resources listed.

All quotes remain the intellectual property of their respective originators. West Wind Fine Art, LLC has received written copyright permission whenever possible and does not asset any claim of copyright for individual quotations. All other use of quotations is done under the fair use principal regarding quotes in the public domain.